THE SUNNY TOP OF CALIFORNIA

The Sunny Top
of California

SIERRA NEVADA POEMS
& A STORY

Norman Schaefer

Norman Schaefer

LA ALAMEDA PRESS :: ALBUQUERQUE

Grateful acknowledgment is made to the editors of VOICES FROM THE AMERICAN LAND: James Burbank, Renny Golden, John Orne Green, Charles E. Little, and Jane Catherwood Sprague, who published some of these poems in the Fall 2009 chapbook, *Bluest Sky*. And to Jerry Reddan of Tangram, who hand-printed "Moonlight on Mt. Ritter" as a broadside in 2008.

Cover image: Chiura Obata—"Clouds, Upper Lyell Trail along Lyell Fork, Sierra, California, 1930," *(detail) woodblock print.*
Used with permission from the Obata family.

Title page image: paw print—wolverine

LIBRARY OF CONGRESS CATALOGING-IN-PUBLICATION DATA:
Schaefer, Norman.
  The sunny top of California : Sierra Nevada poems and a story / Norman Schaefer.
    p. cm.
  ISBN 978-1-888809-58-9
  1. Sierra Nevada (Calif. and Nev.)--Poetry. I. Title.
  PS3619.C3127S86 2010
  811'.6--dc22
                          2010032281

La Alameda Press
9636 Guadalupe Trail NW
Albuquerque, New Mexico 87114

for wolverine

Contents

The ancients loved those poems with natural feel:
Clouds, wind, moon, snow. Flowers, rivers, crags.
A poem should contain strong tempered steel:
Today the poet must learn to lead a charge.

Ho Chi Minh
ON READING THE ANTHOLOGY OF THE TEN THOUSAND POETS
translated by John Balaban

I

BLUEST SKY

Clear Autumn Morning

Orion stalks the Pleiades.
Paper-thin, a silver crescent begins to rise.
Dawn light fills Evolution Basin.
On the southern slopes of Mt. Huxley
folds and wrinkles come into focus.
Cold air drains from Muir Pass.
Frost sparkles on the grasses
white as the Milky Way.
One star by day, thousands at night,
I'm never so alive as here.
I lift a cup of tea to the alpenglow
and clear autumn morning,
alone, happy,
thirty miles from a road.

On Our Way to Red and White Mountain

for Tim Lajcik

Clambering up and around
rugged heaps of talus,
under bluest sky
a long rocky ridge.
We cross a snowy saddle
and Tim speaks of wrestling.
I mention the joys of climbing
in the Buttermilk.
Last night under desert stars
we chattered away
like Douglas squirrels.
Now climbing higher
the mountains have taken
all the words from our mouths.

Night in LeConte Canyon

Moonlight on the Kings,
whitewater rushes up almost to my sleeping bag.
Five days of food
and a good pair of boots,
who can describe my joy?
Silhouettes of cliffs and pines
and all night long the river roar.
Morning will come in blue sky.
I'll cross a snowy pass
and drop down in the Enchanted Gorge.
Ten thousand feet above the business of men,
I place my trust in mountains.

Waking Up on Mt. Winchell

Day breaks over the Inyos.
Venus and the waning crescent moon rise in single file.
I look across at the crooked tooth of Mt. Sill.
In the red dawn Thunderbolt Glacier lies in shadow.
October in the Palisades,
a window of weather without wind or clouds
and warm enough to climb without a shirt.
Now that I'm out of food I'll have to go back down.
This carefree climbing life won't last much longer.
Autumn sunshine will turn to snow
and chase me back to Yolo County.
Saying good⁄by isn't easy.
Rock, wind, ice, sun, snow,
I love them all.
Except for a handful of friends,
where I live I have few connections.
But here on a ledge in the freezing air,
watching the alpenglow light up the peaks,
I feel a part of everything.

Caught in a Thunderstorm

Dark clouds lower the sky,
shrouding Mt. Conness.
Thunder echoes.
Pellets of hail bounce off rocks.
Wind across the tableland
whips my bare legs
and now I've lost my way.
From the rim of Dana Plateau
I can't tell Mono Lake from the sky.

Cold Climb

Biting wind quivers Dade Lake.
Tonight will be cold on Bear Creek Spire.
Ice rims the creeks.
I sense the sun's frustration
spread so thin in autumn.
Following a ridge to the summit,
I am led again far out of myself.
To be on any mountain is privilege enough,
but what would I give tonight
for a shot of Early Times
and my lovely neighbor with me
inside my sleeping bag.
Sometimes it seems I climb mountains
when all I need is down on the ground.
Night wind stings.
Gladly will I welcome the morning star.

On the Summit of Mt. Russell

Pulling up over the last granite blocks
for a view of the colored Kaweahs
and the ragged skyline
of the Great Western Divide.
Puffs of clouds float lazy to the east
and vanish over the dry Owens Valley.
Steep and sheer,
the east face of Mt. Whitney
looms a mile away.
Sitting on the rocky summit,
afternoon sun warms my bare back.
When the mind lets go,
the world's not a problem.
Peaks spread out like flowers in a meadow:
Darwin and Sill far to the north,
dark Minarets hazy beyond.
A flock of rosy-finches
swirls around me like angels.
How can I ever give up the life
of a summer mountaineer?

Another Summer Gone By

The sun rises cold over Thunderbolt Peak.
A layer of frost glitters on my sleeping bag.
Another summer has gone by
and I have nothing to show for it
but idle days adrift in mountains.

Moonlight on Mt. Ritter

Yellow and orange
the autumn moon rises
over the White Mountains.

Bold and enormous
it stands alone
in the dark sky.

White light floods the Minarets,
glimmering upward
from Nydiver Lakes.

Light enough to read
I curl up in my sleeping bag
and open my Kenneth Rexroth:

"The moon hangs in the wide, vacant constellations.
The empty mountains without sound.
The same clear glory extends for ten thousand miles."

Monsoon

Raining again,
the mountains are still wet
from yesterday's storms.
Dark clouds sink in Lost Canyon.
Sawtooth Peak floats in drifting fog
while water runs down the trail
and soaks my shoes.
I feel like a Douglas fir
dripping with rain in the north Cascades,
or a loon yodeling in a cloudburst
on the mouth of the Skagit River.
But don't worry.
I came to the Kaweahs to be alone for a while,
so this monsoon blew in at just the right time.

On the Black Divide

Wind and melting snow,
crumbling spurs.
Boulders scattered like rubbish,
Charybdis: dark, alone.
Plants and animals biding their time,
follow the retreating ice.
Pines march up moraines
warmed by the sun.
Pearl white cumuli
boil overhead.
I climb toward cloudland
everything a-tilt.
Bouldering and mountaineering,
my body gets stronger.
Sleeping by streams,
my mind opens and clears.
Those years of higher learning
at boarding school and college:
better to have spent them here
reading the mountains like a book.

A View from Mt. Sill

I see different mountains I climbed the year before;
days of walking in a glance.
Clyde Minaret or Mt. Clarence King,
where will the next ascent be?
My eyes watch things passing.
We're no sooner born than ground to dust.
Even this slow-paced Sierra will crack and fall apart.
Nothing abides.
For better or for worse,
our lives are as ephemeral as a swarm of mayflies.
One wearing hiking boots
signs his name in the summit register.

At Desolation Lake

A giant moon in thin air
rises over Mt. Humphreys.
Ridges soften in silver light.
Now and then distant rockfall
breaks the silence.
Vanishing breezes make the night more still.
I walk under the triangle
of Deneb, Altair, and Vega
somewhere near the middle.
Arcturus sets while Aldebaran rises,
neighbors on either shore of the sky.
Ten thousand things can break a heart.
Looking for a refuge,
the Sierra Nevada will keep you safe.
How forbidding the world would seem
if there were no mountains to hide away in.
Even if I had handfuls of gold,
I'd rather be poor among these cliffs.

Tehipite

Walking the quiet woods from Crown Valley,
autumn dry grasses crackle underfoot.
California fuchsias bloom bright red.
Yellow jackets buzz by a muddy stream.
I leave the trail and bushwhack south
to the Sierra's largest dome,
and stand on top of Tehipite and look all the way down
to the Middle Fork of the Kings.
A layer of smog newspaper gray hangs low in the west,
pushed by ocean breezes floats slowly this way.
An eagle below soars in the canyon
and I remember Tu Fu:
"The country is ruined,
but the mountains and rivers remain."

Golden Delicious

Aspens yellowing, harsh jay calls,
chilly morning air blows down the canyon.
On a walk today
after two days bouldering in the Buttermilk.
So much to learn,
but tender fingers and elbows must be rested.
A row of gooseberries up a switchback,
the scent of angelica below a crag,
chartreuse lichens glow on dark gorge walls.
Now leaving chickadees and pines
for higher rock
and red-streaked last winter's snow.
Under Middle Palisade Glacier
nap and read in the sun
and bite into an apple all alone,
this golden delicious afternoon.

Gulo Gulo

"Hey mountain lion, get away from that dead deer. I don't care if it's yours; it's mine now and I'm going to eat it. Think I'm joking? Well, you better listen or I'll eat you too.

"I'm the most dangerous animal in the Sierra Nevada. See these legs? They can rip open rotting logs and turn over big rocks. My hind legs are so strong I can't be pushed away, not even by a bear. Look how wide my head is. It's got jaws and teeth inside that will break your bones like chalk. My long curved claws are sharp as razors, and when they cut through that soft underbelly of yours, your guts will drop straight to the ground.

"You're bigger and faster than I am, and you can stalk, but you're not as quick or nearly as mean. I've got the Viking berserk in me. When I fight, I go crazy and don't feel any pain. I never *ever* back off. I'll keep coming at you until you're dead, just like this deer.

"I fear no animal in these mountains. Bears always leave me their food when they see me. They just run off or climb up a tree. But I'm wary of humans with rifles. They've almost killed me off, trapping and hunting me the way they do. I get back at those sons of bitches though. Last week I broke into the ranger's cabin at Charlotte Lake and ate all the bacon, eggs, and powdered milk.

"This carcass is going to spoil, so stop your silly growling and beat it. Next time you'd better remember me because I won't be so patient. I'm Skunk-bear, Carcajou, Glutton. I'm *Gulo gulo,* the wolverine!"

Great Quiet

Dark cliffs surround Miter Basin.
Melting snow fills Sky Blue Lake.
Clear water brings the bright moon near
as it rises above the Corcoran Ridge.
I lie awake in empty soundless mountains,
the brimming lake smooth as glass.
Great quiet grows like an afternoon thunderhead.
If I said anything it could start to rain.

The Lakes Grow Up with Flowers and Trees after the Water Is Gone

Not long ago,
Evolution Meadow was a lake
left by a retreating glacier.
You can see the snowmelt streams
that filled it with sediment
from the slopes above,
making way for grasses and flowers
and finally trees.
A lake might live 10,000 years,
more than a human mind can grasp,
but for Mt. Darwin
rising above Evolution Lake,
it's just another moment
in the lives of streams and glaciers.
In a heartbeat of geologic time
an alpine lake
turns to lodgepole pine forest.
Be careful you don't blink your eyes.

Bolton

Rain and thunder
in the February afternoon,
I sit in the warm kitchen drinking tea
with a large Forest Service map
of the mountains
spread across the table.
A gray short-haired kitten,
Bolton Brown,
flops down on the Kings-Kern Divide
and falls asleep,
his small belly covering
the airy summits of
Mt. Stanford and Mt. Ericcson
that his namesake first climbed in 1896.
A velvet hind leg extends
past foxtail pines and Tyndall Creek
toward huge Mt. Williamson,
another peak he climbed that year,
while a tiny ear points north
to Mt. Clarence King,
his most daring ascent.
He yawns and stretches
and settles down again,
now at rest on the many
shimmering blue lakes

at the headwaters of the Kern River,
rain pouring down outside
as he peacefully dreams
of an earlier life.

Already Old

I walked from Paradise Valley
as far as Upper Basin,
and wobbled in at dusk
ready to drop.
A twenty-mile day,
not bad for a body
already old with scoliosis,
arthritis in a hip,
and tendonitis
in the knee and shoulders.
I'm ready for the marble orchard
and I'm not even 54.
Darkness and all the stars,
the quiet lakes reflecting
the busy city in the sky.
I'll take two codeine
and sleep like a baby,
happy not yet
to wander with a cane.

Lunacy

Quiet as it lifts
over the dark ridge,

a huge white disc,
"a sun from middle earth,"

arching and sailing
in clear cool night.

I wander,
pulled like a tide,

around the lighted water
of Lake South America,

the reflected glow
is never still.

Turning my gaze upward,
searching for the Sea of Tranquility,

a mountain lover
gone mad,

I howl.

New Again

How wonderful finally
to be in the mountains
with nowhere to go.
To sleep late, read,
and walk at my own slow
indolent pace,
not burdened with the thought
of having to climb another peak,
or look for a flower or a bird.
The mind points the feet
and the body follows
like a child.
I'm a beginner again,
a born-again mountain tramp!
Until I run out of food I have everywhere to go.
Resolved: I shall be worthless the whole day,
good for nothing,
a ne'er-do-well,
the shallow end of the gene pool.
Walk on.

Spiller Canyon

II

YELLOW ASPENS

Mt. Stanford

Blue water gathers from a hundred tiny lakes.
Deerhorn Mountain is tall and its peaks are cold.
I need a high place to let my eyes wander.
Lofty summits aren't only for birds.

Tulainyo Lake

I don't carry a camp stove in the mountains.
Nuts and a little dried fruit are plenty enough.
Take a walk above timberline when you're hungry.
The pure air is a meal in itself.

Ediza Lake

When autumn comes it's already freezing in the Minarets.
Take long underwear if your bones rattle like mine.
I remember one night shivering at Iceberg Lake.
Some hells are hot, Buddhists say, but others are cold.

Firebird Ridge

High on a ridge between glaciers,
a rubble of boulders, there's no easy way down.
Lenticular clouds turn dark overhead.
Will the first winter storm bring a poem?

Dade Lake

In autumn it's cold sleeping above the trees.
Slowly at dawn the stars go out in Orion.
Last night I woke the wind blew so hard.
I wonder how many leaves fell off the yellow aspens.

Lamarck Col

Climb Mt. Darwin with a lightweight pack.
Spread your bag out on a slab and crawl inside.
Nibbling on chocolate, gaze up at the Galaxy.
How many shooting stars can you see tonight?

Mt. Williamson

Soft clouds float across the empty sky.
East-flowing streams run hard.
We climb peaks to look out upon the world.
This one almost reaches heaven.

Bubbs Creek

Flooding waterfalls crash against the rocks.
White spray hangs like flowers in the air.
Drink deep this pure mountain water.
Divorce can suck your insides dry.

Mt. Clarence King

Be grateful for your mountaineering life.
Don't climb up what you can't climb down.
A mind that never rests is dangerous.
Just remember: don't be greedy.

Alta Trail

I don't count the years I've come back to the Sierra.
Each spring it's the same old wide and aching sky.
In the fragrant woods I make a bed of pine needles.
I wonder when I'll be old enough to enjoy a motel.

Forester Pass

What has happened to my vitality?
At thirteen thousand feet I can't catch my breath.
When I was twenty, I had a body to die for.
What's left in the mirror looks like chewed gum.

Arrow Peak

Where the river bends a lone mountain soars.
Upside down, it's mirrored in a lake.
Too old for airy ridges, I find pleasure in verse.
A fine poem or a stunning peak: both are equally beautiful.

Spiller Creek

Autumn snow dusts the Sawtooths.
How sad the coming of fall.
A Zen man never regrets the changing seasons.
He doesn't try to braid old whiskers.

Bearpaw Meadow

A meadow in bloom cheers a lone mountaineer.
Looking at mountains, I love mountains more.
This hundred-proof fool sits for a moment free of care.
The earth turns and there's a moon in the sky.

Yosemite Valley

First, azalea blossoms,
then a hermit thrush,
the harvest moon,
and snow—
and the year goes.

Giant Forest

After the bear
attacked me,
Orion looked down
from the sky
as if nothing had happened.

Paiute Pass Trail

Walking out of the mountains,
how can I not think
of Basho's bee
emerging reluctantly
from deep inside a peony?

Polemonium Glacier

An awakened mind
is said
to be priceless,
but how can it compare
with the view from Mt. Sill?

Palisade Glacier

In the late afternoon
the sun has already fallen behind Thunderbolt Peak.
I know dawn will come again,
but how I grow weary
of these long autumn nights.

Tehipite Valley

When I saw a rattlesnake
for the fourth time
this morning,
I became frightened
and ran like an insect.

.

Port Townsend

The Olympics
may be more beautiful,
but the Sierra Nevada is my home range.
A migratory bird
returns to the same tree.

Deer Meadow

Sometimes in the mountains
I feel like a boulder
washed clean in a flooding stream,
and then I'm here,
really here.

Buttermilk Country

At dawn
I keep a watchful eye
on Mt. Tom,
but no amount of guarding
can hold the alpenglow.

Tuolumne Meadows

When you're as old
as I am,
just thinking about the length
of the Muir Trail
can bring you to tears.

Sky Pilots

Either tomorrow
or the day after
they'll bloom,
so I'll wait here
on Forester Pass.

Third Lake

The cherry blossoms on Mt. Yoshino
must be beautiful indeed,
but surely no more than
the Palisades
when they clear after a snowfall.

Ediza Lake

I have wandered
far and wide
in the Sierra Nevada,
but nothing like
the autumn wind tonight.

Rockslide Lake

My shadow
may be as skinny
as a praying mantis,
but it's not afraid
to walk alone.

Lake 11,393

Humming an old Tony Bennett melody
while scrambling over
Thunderbolt Pass,
I look back at North Palisade
where years ago I left my heart.

Bishop Pass

A pipit
sings at dawn
by a nameless lake.
Today looks pretty good
for me too.

Yosemite Valley

This one
dogwood in bloom
is all the spring I need.

Thunderbolt Pass

The snow that fell
like cherry blossoms
is water again.

A clear night on the summit of Mt. Ritter:

If you can't see
the Big Dipper from here
you never will.

Old Army Pass

Even though I wake up
stiff and cold,
dawn breaks anew.

Mono Creek

The horse packer remembers
to drink upstream
with the herd.

Taboose Pass Trail

Tasting wild currants
all dark and sweet by the trail—
first autumn snow.

Colby Meadow

What has the butterfly
lost in the meadow
that it keeps looking for?

Paradise Valley

On a moonlit boulder
the shadow
of a bear.

Highway 395

Autumn snowfall:
even the nameless peaks
get decorated.

Onion Valley

Sometimes a cricket
is all you need
for a night to exist.

Mirror Lake

Just like that
spring came to Yosemite
in a deep blue sky.

Glen Pass

When the snow melts,
Rae Lakes Basin
overflows with hikers.

North Fork of Lone Pine Creek

An aspen leaf
never falls
in vain.

Hamilton Lakes

Even if the river dries up,
there will be a little stream
to float away on.

Sawtooth Pass

How do you learn
a range of mountains?
With an open heart and your feet too.

Forester Pass

May I roam
as a ghost someday
these summer mountains again.

III

BEAR LESSONS

Bear Lessons

Waiting for the Great One

Constellations move across Yosemite.
The moon drops behind dark pines.
It is foolish to stay awake the night.
The bear will show himself when he pleases.

I wrote this brief poem a few summers ago after climbing Mt. Clark in Yosemite National Park. It came to me early the following morning at Merced Lake where I'd spent the night. A little later I got lucky. Walking through the quiet woods near Lost Valley, I watched a black bear *(Ursus americanus)* and her two cubs ford the Merced River and then disappear into the forest. That for me was as good as topping out on Mt. Clark, one of my favorite Yosemite peaks. Drawn to bears as much as mountains, I get just as excited seeing them now as I did the first time, when I watched one near Echo Summit lope across Highway 50 nearly thirty-five years ago.

But early last Halloween morning my luck changed unexpectedly, or so it seemed. Sleeping at the edge of Crescent Meadow in Sequoia National Park, I was there not to begin a mountaineering trip, but just to wander through Giant Forest a few days, enjoy the ancient sequoias, and see, I hoped, some bears.

Bears resemble us. When they reach for acorns or berries, they often stand upright, like us, on the soles of their feet, and if you ignore their claws, their hind paw prints match our footprints. Their heavy pelts add to their hulking shapes, making them more burly than we, but they are neither clumsy nor slow. Surprisingly agile and graceful, they climb rocks and trees with aplomb, contradicting their somewhat portly appearances. Bears' claws are delicate and precise. They can pick up and rotate an acorn with two tips and in captivity have been known to peel peaches. There is even a well-documented case of a bear escaping from a locked cage by carefully picking the lock with a single dexterous claw. Just like us, bears are mammals, who are hot, hairy, sometimes smell, and have sour breath. They give birth to blind, helpless, nearly naked young, who are no bigger than a squirrel and weigh less than a pound, and carefully tend and nurse them on mother's milk. A biologist once said that human beings are the only animals that can run or walk many miles, swim across a river, and then climb a tree, but he forgot the bear, who can do them all faster and with greater endurance. Bears woo with affection, moan and sigh when they worry, snore, spank their cubs (who play tag, roughhouse, and somersault while holding their feet), keep tidy dens, and enjoy hot tubs and sweets. They can be moody, gruff, and morose. Bears love to loaf. I have watched them lounge in mountain meadows, chewing stems of lupines and shooting stars for most of a summer afternoon. They are intelligent, curious, have long memories, and are tolerant of humans. Cubs in captivity enjoy riding in backpacks; adults like traveling by truck. The Ojibway of the Lake Superior region often called bears *anijinabe,* their word for Indian, and in the arid Southwest the Yavapai say, "Bears are like people except they can't make fire." They are a reminder of what we might have become if we hadn't left the wilderness for cities.

In late October nights get chilly in the Sierra Nevada, and they get longer. Lying in a sleeping bag for thirteen or fourteen hours isn't uncommon, but it's hard to sleep straight through. That night, however, I did well, only waking up once, and after reading a while—a dog-eared copy of Kenneth Rexroth's *One Hundred Poems from the Chinese*—I turned off my flashlight and looked up at the stars. Orion, high in the southern sky, told me that dawn wasn't more than two hours below the horizon. Night had passed faster than I thought. The sudden chirp of a small bird, maybe one of several species of warblers who would soon be leaving for warmer winter climes, offered a clue that an animal was around. Shortly after, I heard water splash. It sounded louder, I thought, than the more cautious splash a deer usually makes entering a stream, so I was pretty sure a bear was close by. I wasn't alone, but it didn't matter. Black bears have wandered into my campsites many times before and have never been a problem. Tonight there was no food in my camp (I'd put it in a bear-proof storage box), so I curled deep in my sleeping bag, covering my head, and fell back asleep unconcerned.

Not more than a few minutes later came a surprise I wouldn't forget for a long time: a bear jumped on me. Its curved, almost catlike claws, sharpened by constant contact with granite, stream gravels, dirt, sand, and tree bark cut all the way through my sleeping bag, wool sweater, and long underwear and scraped my back. Like a fish to a hook my mind rose to the fact that a bear was on my back, and instinctively I rolled over, faced him, and yelled "Bear!" as loudly as I could. In the Sierra making loud noises like shouting or beating an iron frying pan with a long-handled spoon, usually chases a bear away, but when he didn't move it was "root hog or die," and I grabbed the thick coarse fur below his throat and tried to push him off. For someone weighing less than 150 pounds this was folly. He was too heavy and too strong to shove more than a foot or two, but it was enough to get my legs out of my sleeping bag and stand up. Escaping, however, didn't come without a price. As we wrestled, the bear got a taste of my right arm, biting it, as I later saw at a hospital, clear to the bone. And time was in slow motion when one of his knife-edged nails neatly sliced part of my lower lip, leaving it dangling from my mouth. Less than a minute before I was sound asleep.

As a little boy growing up in the fifties in Olympia, Washington, I played in the woods and swamps near our house. No bears were there, but they already lurked in my imagination. After kindergarten on afternoons when it rained, my mother often read me "Goldilocks and the Three Bears," Grimm's "Snow White and Rose Red," and *Winnie the Pooh.* On my bed was a large cinnamon brown teddy with whom I talked and slept at night. I was sure a bear was behind the hot water heater in our next door neighbor's basement, and that another one lived in the thick blackberry patch in our back yard. At my grandmother Jesse's boardinghouse on Capitol Way, I remember sitting on her lap and listening to "The Teddy Bear's Picnic," playing on her Victrola. We ate fresh bear claw pastries together that she bought for a dime apiece at Koehler's Bakery across the alley. Big, aloof, confident, and sometimes rough, even my brother seemed like a bear. My sister soon went off to Mills College in Oakland, and it was from her that I first heard of beatniks, Berkeley, and the California Golden Bears. There were other bears in Los Angeles, my father told me, called the UCLA Bruins, and Ernie Banks was hitting home runs for the Chicago Cubs. Olympia High School's mascot was the bear, and fifty miles west on the Washington coast was Olympia

High's arch rival, the Hoquiam Grizzlies. Riding on Highway 99 with my mother and father, I saw Smokey the Bear on billboards from Bellingham to Grants Pass, but it wasn't until the late sixties as a student at the University of California at Davis that I walked into the Tahoe Sierra and saw some real bears. Now almost fifty-five, I was suddenly sitting at the "bear's end of the table." My Halloween was getting off to an unusual start.

Surprised at how tall I was when I got on my feet, the bear climbed quickly up a white fir next to my camp and peered down at me. Getting a view of the whole bear for the first time, I saw that he had black fur (black bears in the western United States can also have blond, cinnamon, or brown coats), looked thick and heavy from a good feeding season, but didn't appear quite fully grown. Nevertheless, he was impressive. As is the fate of juvenile black bears, his mother had probably sent him up a tree his second summer and walked away, putting him in danger of mountain lions, rattlesnakes, fire, automobiles, and especially big male bears, who would kill and eat him if given the opportunity. Following the seasonal forage, he most likely had picked up a few scars from clashes with cranky adults working out their pecking order. In the foraging hierarchy sub-adult bears are always at the bottom. Now bigger and more experienced after having lived several years, he had an excellent chance of reaching full maturity.

The bear climbed gracefully down about a minute later. Apparently attracted to a smell in my sleeping bag, he went right over to it and began clawing it frantically. Made by Mountain Hardware, I'd had the bag for three years and used it in the mountains more than thirty times. In the morning I often ate breakfast in it and dinner when it was cold. He could have caught a whiff of the nuts and dried fruit I always have with me on mountain trips. Sweets, like meat, rank high on the list of a black bear's food choices. If not the scent of food or duck down feathers, it might have been my own, which can get ripe in the high country. I've never liked laundering a down sleeping bag because it loses its warmth. I'd rather just air it out after I've used it. Whatever odor drew him, it's hard to imagine the keenness of a black bear's nose, which can detect a human being a mile upwind and a carcass at ten. A short Native American poem describes a bear's acute sense of smell very well:

> A pine needle fell.
> The eagle saw it.
> The deer heard it.
> The bear smelled it.

I would miss my bag. Lightweight but warm, it had been with me on some of my best mountaineering trips, like one on the Kings-Kern Divide, when camped for the night on Forester Pass after climbing Junction Peak, I could smell in the dark the fragrant, musky, rock-ledge gardens of blue *Polemonium eximium*, sky pilot, just before falling off to sleep more than thirteen thousand feet above the sea. At night I read stories and poems inside it, was always comfortable, and had good dreams. The bear was in a frenzy and ruined my sleeping bag so quickly that there was no reason to toss rocks at him, another effective tactic in the Sierra to make a bear go away. So I stepped back and tried to collect myself while he went on tearing it up. My mind was reeling from the shock of being attacked in my sleep by a bear, which I'd never heard happen in the Sierra Nevada, especially when no food was around.

I was wounded and I was afraid, but I couldn't help noticing how clear and present everything was around me. The bear, his sharp, sour smelling fur, the stars, trees, and pale sliver of moon rising above them were unbelievably vivid, and I thought of Van Gogh's "Starry Night." I was alive and warm, and despite the beating I'd taken, didn't feel any pain. My body was wired with adrenalin.

When he stopped his raking, the bear turned around and walked toward me. He could attack again and that scared me, but maybe he wouldn't. If he had wanted to kill me, he could have easily the first time, either by biting my neck or slicing it open with his claws, but instead he ran up the tree when I got free of my bag and stood up. And he wasn't huffing or bellowing hoarsely, walking in a stiff-legged gait, or slapping the ground with his forepaws, common signs that a bear is going to charge. So I stayed where I was, and when he approached about ten feet away, I yelled in a voice I didn't recognize, "Get out of here, bear! Go away!" To my great relief he turned back around, ambled over to my sleeping bag again, and completely shredded it. The bear took to the tattered thing like a cat to catnip, and once when he shook it furiously in his jaws, soft, tiny feathers rose and fell around him like snow. A park ranger later told me that the bear had dragged its remains into Crescent Meadow.

An old-time woodsman from Northern Michigan once told Ben East, field editor for *Outdoor Life,* "A bear will eat anything a hog will eat and some things a hog won't look at." To be sure, almost anything a black bear's paws can reach serves as food: clover, wildflowers, snails, caterpillars, mice, dandelions, acorns, pine nuts, bird eggs, cambium, mushrooms (feeding so heavily on them that his feces turn whitish), frogs, grasshoppers, crickets, crayfish, manzanita berries, thimbleberries, currants, carrion, and cultivated corn. He will spend hour after hour turning over rocks and breaking apart logs for protein-rich hornets, wasps, yellow jackets, a variety of bees, berries, and ants. No beehive is safe. He may smash open a half a dozen in a single foray. Black bears love apples, eating huge quantities and barely chewing them, and any Yosemite visitor who has ever watched one ransack the apple orchard at Curry Village will agree that no one is more adept at climbing into an apple tree and raking or shaking down the fruit. For a black bear the mountains are, to quote Milton, a "wildernesse of sweets." About eighty percent of his diet is plant material. The biggest omnivore, he will eat anything except, as John Muir once said, granite. He is a skillful scavenger, a bona fide second-story man, who has tasted everything found in cabins, ranger huts, barns, ice chests, food lockers, tents, RVs, and campground dumpsters, often seen hightailing it into the woods with his face covered with honey, molasses, flour, or bacon grease. Beginning in late summer, the black bear's feeding pace accelerates to as much as 20,000 calories a day (what wildlife biologists call hyperphagia) as it harvests fruit, nuts, and acorns, putting on weight at a remarkable rate, sometimes several pounds a day. Picking whatever is ripe, killing when necessary, the black bear's personality is largely shaped by his willingness to eat almost anything. His vast, unrestricted bill of fare is what makes the whole world interesting to him, and in *The Sacred Paw* Paul Shepard and Barry Sanders say that it's his "broad, searching, persistent openness" in the way he explores the mountains that makes us recognize the bear in ourselves.

Satiated at last, he disappeared into the trees. By my ravaged bag were my pack, a pair of sandals, a couple of books, a flashlight, and my glasses, none of which the bear had touched. But my glasses, which I needed for driving, were broken. I must have stepped on them after wrestling my way out of my sleeping bag. Thinking I'd just have to squint my eyes and drive slowly, I gathered up my gear with my good arm and then the food out of the storage container. But just as I started for my pickup, luckily only 150 or so yards away, the bear re-emerged and began walking alongside me at about twenty feet. I didn't mind him much being so close now because I believed it was my sleeping bag he was after, not me. And I didn't think he was mean or a "rogue bear" either. He was, I thought, just curious in the way bears are from their first outing onward. Not all campground bears are after only food. Still, it was so odd that he grabbed my bag with me asleep inside and no food nearby. Maybe I had it coming. Teachers of the old ways tell us that creatures feel embarrassed when watched or talked about and may be offended by a careless gesture or word. An Athapaskan elder of the Yukon, for example, might tell his grandchildren that it's rude to point at a raven. Perhaps this big fellow had finally come to remind me. Even today when I see a bear, I watch it as long as I can, often as amazed as I was the first time I saw one. It's impolite to stare, but with bears I've never been able to help myself.

As I was putting my stuff in the truck, I noticed I'd left one of my sandals behind. It was the left half of a new pair of Chacos, the most comfortable pair of sandals I've ever worn, excellent for wandering in the mountains, on trails or off, and even adequate on moderately difficult climbing routes. Too cheap to leave it behind, I sighed and plodded back in the dark, and the artless bear quietly tagged along, always keeping abreast of me about fifteen or twenty feet. After I found the sandal, I looked a last time at my wasted bag. In the back country it's good to leave as little sign as possible of your passing through, but the Park Service would have to clean up the mess of scattered down feathers. I kneeled down by the ragged garnet-colored sleeping bag cover, and the bear moved in close, surely thinking it was now his. When I waved it to back him off, I spooked him, and he shot up the fir again. But he was back down in a few seconds, composed, and patiently walking by me back to my truck. Here was a creature completely at home in the forests of the Sierra Nevada, the "top animal," as ecologists say, who knew where everything was in the mountains and how to get there. I watched the easy, confident way he moved and wished I had a coat like his.

The adrenalin was leaving my system, and I began to feel some pain, but I couldn't help also becoming aware of the irony, the humor, and the beauty of the bear and I walking slowly together back and forth, an odd couple in an odd procession, silently passing in and out of shadows, stars shimmering in the cold night sky. I was beginning to see him now as my "animal shadow," a natural cousin in a fur coat, not only stronger and faster, but more clever and free than I, a hairless primate, living in the gray world of cities. Carl Jung speaks of a bear with shining eyes deep in the human unconscious, the wild inside us. Something was happening and I wanted to stay, but I needed to find a hospital. Without thinking to say goodbye, I turned on the lights and started the engine, and watched the bear disappear into the woods.

The General's Highway looked blurred without my glasses, and my right arm couldn't shift very well, but I kept squinting and before long was creeping down 180, the meandering Kings Canyon Highway. Leaving one world for another, sometimes stopping for deer, I felt strangely open, beat up as I was. But by the time I reached Centerville and its beautiful groves of valley oaks, my arm had come out of shock and hurt more, and my legs were shaking. Even so, life was full of promise again because it was getting light, I'd stopped bleeding, and was only fifteen or twenty miles from downtown Fresno where I could get sewed up. I stopped at a bus stop on Ventura Street and asked a man where the nearest hospital was. He spoke Spanish, and when he saw the blood on my face and clothes, pointed to a traffic light down the street and gestured to turn right. *"No lejos,"* he said, *"no lejos,"* meaning "not far away." Soon I found it, the University Medical Center, and checked into Emergency, where I was X-rayed, stitched, bandaged, and injected against tetanus and rabies. I was lucky; there was no tendon or nerve damage in my arm, and it wasn't broken. And I still had full use of my fingers. The care I was given was good. Shootings and stabbings were down that night, so I never waited long. Even my glasses were glued back together. A supervisor told me I was the ER's first bear attack victim, and friendly, curious doctors, interns, and nurses stood around my bed asking me questions.

Meanwhile my wife, Ruth, worried at home in Old East Davis. She was either sleeping or taking a shower when I left a message that I'd been attacked by a bear and was in a hospital, but I was goofing so badly that I forgot to tell her what hospital and city I was in. She couldn't get my number from the phone's callback feature because I'd called from a different area code. Getting more anxious, Ruth called the phone company and asked to trace my call, but they wouldn't do it. After I registered, I left word at Sacramento State, where she teaches, and this time remembered to tell her the name of the hospital. Not long after, she got in touch. I've troubled her before when I was in the mountains. Once after a few days climbing above the headwaters of the North Fork of Big Pine Creek, I called from

Big Pine to let her know I was fine, and that the body that had just been pulled out of a crevasse in the Palisade Glacier wasn't mine, but someone else's. Now almost noon, I upset her again as I sped north across the dry San Joaquin Valley for home. Ruth insisted I stay in Fresno a day or two with some painkiller and her taking care of me, but what I wanted was our bed and some of her homemade vegetable soup. I was driving one-handed (my right arm was in a sling) on old, rundown Highway 99, risky enough with both hands on the wheel, but it was worth it. To the east, blotted out by smog, were the mountains and the bear. What was he up to, I wondered.

My dream life was rich the first few nights back home. One dream in particular I had twice. I was sitting on a cliff overlooking a wide grassland that teemed with large mammals from every part of the world. A great exuberant mix, they were all running together: jaguars, zebras, polar bears, tigers, caribou, cheetahs, pronghorn, kangaroos, giraffes, rhinos, elephants, and more. In brilliant color the immense herd kept coming, galloping from one end of the plain to the other. This dream was good medicine, and I woke up each time feeling exhilarated.

There were periods of longing too and grateful tears. The bear made me feel truly alive. In a few seconds he'd stripped me of every pretense I had about myself, and for a moment without anything I was really there. When you know you're a fool, you can live in the world. The bit of clarity I experienced didn't last for long, but the bear had knocked some sense into me, or at least it seemed. How true the harm one comes upon is often a gift.

Two weeks later my stitches have been removed, and there are new scars on my arms that I'll brag shamelessly about for the rest of my life. I'm still getting rabies shots, but they're painless because you don't take them in the belly anymore. My right arm still isn't as strong as my left, but I'm working again, gardening and raking leaves. After long, hot, summer drought, autumn is a pleasant time to work in the Sacramento Valley. Friends have called, sent word, or come to visit. And someone told the local newspaper, who sent a reporter and a photographer over. Part of being in the mountains, I guess, means having a good story to tell when you come back home.

Wilderness is full of surprise, where the uncommon happens. No one more than the bear, whom I still miss, has so clearly reminded me of my own, and everyone else's, frailty and transience. Nor has anyone made me more aware that the realm of human and animal is the same. Like the mountain lion, who can also kill us and eat us, the black bear helps us appreciate our own impermanence and gives us a needed modesty and grounding when we walk through the forest. (Indians believed that bears were sent down to Earth to teach men humility.) We are, after all, no more and no less than another being on the planet and in a way just passing through. I doubt that I could have learned these lessons from a book, or a lecture, or even on a cushion in a meditation hall. Arrogance and stubbornness have been my curse, so I learn mostly from stumbling. But I don't regret how this instruction came about. In fact, I am deeply touched that an animal, especially a bear, would come forward, give me the cuffing up I needed, and send me home a little worse for wear maybe, but hopefully more awake. In June when the snow has melted, I'll be going back to Giant Forest for the Big Trees and the dogwoods in bloom. Maybe the bear and I will meet again. Hopefully I won't be sleeping, but that's not for me to say. The bear will show himself when he pleases.

·

I returned to Giant Forest at the end of June. Claw marks were distinct on the white fir the bear had twice climbed, and to my surprise down feathers were still strewn about. I walked a few hours through the woods admiring the wise old sequoias, and, still staring, a beautiful cinnamon-colored sow, lounging by a stream with her two cubs. When I came back, some Japanese girls no older than ten or eleven gathered where the bear and I had briefly wrangled. I watched them as they joined hands and danced in a circle, sometimes stomping their feet where the bear had pounced on me, while their parents sat and chatted nearby. Some of them wore their hair in pigtails, and they laughed in delight as they leapt and danced. A new event was scratching out an old one. So this is how this story ends, I thought, and I was laughing too.

IV

FRIEND MOON

The Sunny Top of California

Dew gathers on the meadow grasses.
Deneb takes its place in the center of the sky.
Step by step around Rockslide Lake,
keeping my eyes on the radiant moon,
I call out the names of old Chinese poets,
who instruct me by saying nothing.
All my life I've loved high lonesome places.
Odors of moss and bark
and cones and twigs and snowmelt mud,
I feel like I've been coming to the Sierra Nevada
for a thousand years.
A human life is no more than a flicker of lightning,
but to die on a glacier
my bones would be pure forever.
Watching the moon begin its slow descent,
my mind quiets down
until there's scarcely a ripple.
In the morning I'll look for a campsite
somewhere green and steep and wild
where a wolverine might feel safe.
I talk brave,
but all I want is an autumn alone with books and tea
and Bugler cigarettes rolled-your-own,
to be deeply enjoyed without hurry
on the sunny top of California.

Up and Down the Black Kaweah

Tiny needles of cold rain.
Twilight darkens Black Rock Pass.
In gray dawn I started up alone,
the low moon hazy over Eagle Scout Peak.
When the sun was overhead
I had picked my way down
nervous, old, and tottery rock
and followed a trail out of Big Arroyo.
Clouds open to stars.
If you'll kindly move, mosquitoes,
I'd like to sleep.
Damp, tired,
but still in one piece,
this summer eve by a lake.

Ritter Range

Streams rush down bringing water from the glaciers.
Bows to the maker of this desolate scene:

ragged pinnacles looming dark and steep,
bucks with velvet antlers crossing rocky slopes.

Clear blue sky goes a hundred miles.
With each step up pure wind rises.

Surrender and stretch out like the world.
Whoever sees these mountains is stunned.

after Hồ Xuân Hương, 18th century

Blisters

Making my way up a muddy footpath
past flower gardens and shrubs,
birds call above the stream roar.
Beyond a slope of pines Deerhorn Mountain,
but I won't be climbing it today.
A raw blister throbs on my heel,
another on a toe.
I shuffle along,
leave the boot untied.
On my knees I look at different tiny flowers,
ponder racers and yellow-legged frogs,
and find butterflies I've never seen.
A cinnamon-colored bear sits
in a creek shallow.
Sunlight flickers on a redtail soaring.
Watching caddisfly larvae
walk along a stream bottom,
little rainbows in a blue-green pool;
a hummer likes my fading red hair.
I should get blisters more often.
Eating lunch in a field of penstemon,
a sunny bath in Lake Reflection.

Meeting Norman Clyde

I was spreading out my sleeping bag by Upper Boy Scout Lake when I saw Norman Clyde.

"Norman," I said, "you've been dead for thirty years. Your ashes were scattered in the Palisades."

"Yeah, things didn't work out in paradise. There was nothing to do; I just lay around in bliss. Now all my calluses from cutting wood are gone." Then he showed me his hands, large but soft and pink like a baby's.

"I need a struggle to feel alive; something to believe in that's bigger than myself. Mountains always gave me that and so I came back."

Climbing North Palisade

Dawn in the mountains,
the pale half moon drops in the Enchanted Gorge.
Pink haze blurs the horizon.
A breeze chills my skin while I put on clothes.
Trudging up the dark gully,
eerie cliffs still in shadow,
loose rock and sand slip underfoot.
Water drips off the catwalk.
Falling rocks tumble and echo.
Climbing a crack to a ledge,
scrambling up summit boulders
as big as houses.
Beyond mountains,
mountains.
Sometimes a mystery
is better than an answer.

Caveat

My stubble grows white
among a hundred granite peaks.
Passions are never easily put aside.
Edging across a narrow arête,
manteling an airy summit block;
the same thing that makes you live
can kill you in the end.

Palisade Creek

Loafing

Easy to be happy here
loafing in streamside shade,

nutcrackers call
in the warm woods

but quiet in Miter Basin
where few ever go.

Blue lakes with golden trout,
meadows and all their flowers,

granite that won't break
when you pull down hard.

A sleeping bag, some food,
and a poncho if it rains:

everything you need is with you.
Everywhere you go is home.

In Ionian Basin

My mother always worried
when I went to the mountains,

saying call when you come back,
not before you go.

In an amphitheater of moonlit lakes and peaks
I lie awake thinking of her.

Short of breath her final days,
barely able to walk.

Now a ghost
she tramples the sky.

Even the Wind That Chills to the Bone
Is a Pleasure

Lightning shooting out of their bellies,
cloud dragons collapse on the Great Western Divide.
Sweeps of rain drag across Center Basin.
Peak after peak loses its light.
Shivering wet, I've forgotten my rain gear again.
How could I be so absent-minded?
Still, I'm buzzed, as high as a hummingbird.
Moments like these you can still love the mountains.

Re/entry

After wandering a few weeks
in the southern Sierra,
it's strange to sleep in a room
without animals or stars.
Hard too to feel comfortable again
with the tame sounds of a household:
the ring of a telephone, the flush of a toilet,
water running in the sink, a knock on the door.
Re/entry isn't easy.
No amount of wine seems to help.
I guess I'm still a sub/adult
who's only happy when he's off alone somewhere
walking in the mountains.
More than a week late getting home,
I spent last night again at Charlotte Lake.
You can't hear too much of wind in the pines.

Upper Basin

One year in fall
I lived a month on these ridges.
Now I wander through again
a mere passerby.
These lakes and cliffs
still remember me,
and the blue sky
that returns after a snowfall
offers me once more
what's left of summer.

after Muso Soseki, 13th century

o for 4

At Deer Meadow last night
I lay awake in my sleeping bag
waiting for a poem
until Pegasus was rising in the sky.
Full of hope the night before on Knapsack Pass,
I stayed up and watched Antares set,
but heard no song in the air.
A mirror image of Arrow Peak
reflects upside down on Bench Lake:
try, try, and again, but no poem comes.
Will I strike out too tomorrow
camping in Sixty Lakes Basin?
Keep swinging, pal.
Even Dimaggio went 0 for 4.

No Place to Entertain Family or Friends

At Tyndall Basin's highest lake
nothing much goes on.
A few puffs of passing clouds,
a marmot dozing on a rock,
are about all that's happening.
The nearest pines are a thousand feet below.
All morning long in boulder shade
I nap and read in my sleeping bag.
Maybe later I'll get up and go for a walk.
I always enjoy myself at Lake 12,460,
but it's no place to entertain family or friends.
What more could I offer them
but this fragrance of sky pilot,
this taste of clear running water?

Wishful Thinking Tonight

I prefer a quiet place,
but love sleeping by this murmuring stream.
Above me Ursa Major circles the North Star.
Arcturus falls on the Black Divide.
They say Old Honey Paws
has always come to Little Pete Meadow.
If I'm lucky he'll visit again tonight.
We'll sit together by the river
or maybe follow it in the moonlight
as it turns and tumbles down to Tehipite Valley.
He'll let me in on all the gossip,
like where the acorn harvest is,
what kind of winter to expect,
or where a hollow log might be for a den.
Pride and beauty of the forest
covered in his friendly fur robe,
without bears the world wouldn't be a world.
Honor the gods,
but a fool who trusts them
had better be careful.
I make a place beside me for the Venerable One
and hang my food from the highest pine.

Blue Chip

One hundred trips in the Sierra
and I'm still coming back,

though forgetful at times
to bring map or poncho

and more than once not remembering
the way I came.

Each peak,
every flower,

from now on
it's all clear profit.

I live like a Rockefeller
in these mountains

whether I know where I am
or not.

What Will I Do

What will I do when I'm old and harmless
and can't go into the mountains anymore?
Well, I'd like to get better at birding.
In Uptown I know the birds pretty well by sight,
but not many by their calls.
I should sharpen up on my botany too.
Except for trillium and lady's slipper
I doubt I know any of the wildflowers
growing in the woods at Fort Worden.
Tree sitting is a noble activity
and Earth First! down in Humboldt County
is always looking for volunteers.
A tiny platform high in an old-growth redwood
is no place to get dizzy,
but I think I'd do fine.
Probably the greatest pleasure though
will just come from reading my poems
about the Sierra Nevada.
I have several manuscripts of them;
little songs and longer ones
each one neatly typed on a crisp white page.
Getting wet, getting cold, getting bitten by a bear;
the joyous hardship of climbing a peak
for a clear far view.
So many experiences lying on my lap,

if my creative skills haven't gone to seed,
I might even make some revisions.
Sipping whiskey and saying my poems out loud,
I'll make sure every phrase is alive,
like *Howl,* like *Riprap,* like *Scrambled Eggs and Whiskey.*
I won't accept one dead word.
Then it will be like re-living those old wild times—
right here in my rocker.

What the Trail Crew Boss Said
about the Harvest Moon

"Oh, she's kinda shy all right blushin' the way she
does when she's first peekin' over them mountains,
but you got to understand, son, she only comes
out once a year. Still, she ain't bashful for long.
Hell, by the time she's in the middle of the sky,
ain't none of us'll be able to sleep."

All the Way to the Bank

In the world of business
I never came into my own.
My wealth is wind in the pines,
the moon over peaks.
So many walks among them
have taught me to love even mist and rain.
In upper LeConte Canyon
spring wildflowers add warmth to sunlight.
Whitewater on the Kings
roars like Beethoven's "Ode to Joy."
Sometimes my mind feels weightless
and without color.
To the awakened eye,
they say in Zen,
streams and mountains completely disappear.
Raking leaves or cutting wood
doesn't bring in much money,
but that's okay.
After a night by Wanda Lake
I'm laughing all the way to the bank.

By an Unnamed Lake

Flicks of lightning nicking the horizon
spark a difficult mind.
Mountains around me for neighbors,
rosy-finches to help me sing,
whatever I see enters into me;
I drink it in.
Awareness blossoms everywhere.
This lake knows I'm here.
I thought I heard a voice on Diamond Mesa:
"Forget yourself and you're free."

Thanks to Yvon Chouinard

Why, I don't know,
but at the end of October
the Sawtooth Ridge is as cold as anywhere
in the High Sierra.
Fifteen years ago,
standing on the summit of Matterhorn Peak,
the sky was so chill and clear
Mt. Conness seemed only half as far away.
Looking back, I wonder how I did it:
those lean autumns climbing in Levi's
blown out in the seat and knees,
and hand-me-down sweaters
bought for a song at St. Vincent de Paul.
I always wore cotton and wool then.
So, lucky me to be perched again
on this ridge at dawn.
I can't climb worth a damn anymore,
but I sure am toasty warm
dressed in my capilene long underwear
and Patagonia fleece.

Haboku

My legs are tired,
but my eyes feel refreshed.

Following Rock Creek in rain and fog,
it's one splendid alpine scene after another.

But hard to tell on New Army Pass
if it's real or a painting—

the dark ink of ravens,
the pale wash of peaks.

Looking East, Looking West:
Following the North Fork of Big Pine Creek from Glacier Lodge

A rose is blooming over the dark desert mountains.
Just over there dawn is coming.
Then a glimpse of the Palisades rising above the glaciers,
pink as a watermelon's heart.
Already I'm blown away by the joyous pulse of mountains.
Each spring, it seems,
the Sierra Nevada shines brighter than ever.
Everywhere again soft breezes and warm sunshine;
the morning stands up straight.
Sunburn on my face, blisters on my feet,
I walk again;
the tread on my boots good for another thousand miles.
Though I'm beginning to fall apart at the seams,
I feel full of victory.
Above timberline I'm more free to feel, think, and say.
I light a stick of incense on the Palisade Glacier
grateful for the life that remains to me
and the luck of finding these mountains.
Drifting freely in this house of fresh air,
out of touch with the world's rise and fall,
I sometimes hear the words of Muso Soseki:
"Traveling east or west, light and free on the one road,
I don't know if I'm on the way or at home."

Memories

Whenever I come down from the mountains,
they always give me something
to remember them by.
The greater my gratitude,
it seems,
the greater their gift.
For example six years ago
when I reached the top of Mt. Winchell,
a cold October morning at dawn,
I drove home with a cliff
the size of a hotel.
Or one September
after walking the Muir Trail,
I hitchhiked north from Lone Pine
with a hundred feet of Bubbs Creek.
And when I left Yosemite last night,
I was given a dozen fragrant Jeffrey pines
after the exquisite stillness I felt
sitting alone by the Tuolumne River.
Memories of mountains
big enough to walk into
and stay awhile.
Maybe one day
I won't have to leave home.

Friend Moon

Friend moon, hello again.
I have watched you from hundreds of places
hundreds of nights,
and here where marmots do their perfect work
you bring me my shadow.
Unhurried, steady,
you float up above Mt. Williamson.
In the free air and free spaces
there is always room enough
and time enough.
Your cool light strangely arouses
and I see why Li Po is said
to have embraced you in a river.
Aspens turn again.
Soon these silver peaks will be dusted with snow
and deer will walk down the dry east slope.
How much I value your companionship.
Shall we meet next spring when the larkspurs bloom
and the good bears prowl the sweet-scented woods?

Norman Schaefer lives in Port Townsend, Washington. *The Sunny Top of California*, which was written from 1994/2009, is his first book of poetry. He still visits the Sierra Nevada every year.

COLOPHON

Set in Poliphilus, a typeface issued by Stanley Morison for Monotype
in 1922, based on the text of the *Hypnerotomachia Poliphili*
published by Aldus Manutius in Venice in 1499. The face actually
reproduces the irregularities of fifteenth century printing
on dampened handmade paper with its inky spread.
The italic is Blado designed by the
calligrapher Ludovico degli Arrighi.

•

Book Design :: JB Bryan